THE SCIENCE OF DEVELOPMENT Part 1

(LECTURE NOTES SERIES)

UWEM ESSIA

TABLE OF CONTENTS

TABLE OF CONTENTS

Introduction

CHAPTER ONE

   DEVELOPMENT AND GROWTH ECONOMICS

      1.1. Growth Vs Development Economics

      1.2. Development Economics

   A. Effect of colonization

   B. The effect of cultural heterogeneity

   C. Human capacity

   1.3. Globalization of development

   1.4. Common Terms Used in Modern Development Studies

      A. Underdeveloped Countries

      B. North and South Countries

      C. Third World

CHAPTER TWO

   MARXISM AND DEVELOPMENT

      2.1. The Forces of Production

      2.2. The Importance of Ideology to Development

      2.2.1. Material Vs Idealistic Determinism

      2.3. Economic Development Vs Development

      2.3.1. Lessons from China's experiences

      2.3.2. Lessons from the experience of the Defunct Soviet Union

      2.4. Marxism in Contemporary Development Thought

CHAPTER THREE
ROSTOW'S STAGES OF GROWTH THEORY

CHAPTER FOUR
HARROD-DOMAR MODEL
4.1. Mathematical Presentation

CHAPTER FIVE
SOLOW–SWAN MODEL
5.1. Mathematics of the S-S Model
5.2. Mankiw–Romer–Weil Version S-S Model

CHAPTER SIX
JOSEPH SCHUMPETER'S THEORY OF DEVELOPMENT
Relevance of Schumpeter's Theory for Developing Countries:

CHAPTER SEVEN
DEVELOPMENT STRATEGIES
7.1. Inward Vs Outward Looking development Strategies
7.2. Import Substitution Industrialization (ISI) Vs Export Promotion Strategy
7.3. The missing-Component Approach and Development Diagnostics

CHAPTER EIGHT
POVERTY AND INEQUALITY
8.1. Poverty inducing Factors
8.2. Poverty and the agrarian system in Africa

Introduction

Development is commonly described as the overall improvement in the wellbeing of persons, improvement in the functioning of systems and institutions, and the attainment of positive peace. Economic development is a significant aspect of overall development but by no means all of it. For instance, factors like social cohesion, cultural modernization, good neighborliness, and strong civil societies, among others are essential for development but lack economic measures.

This Lecture Notes Series on the Science of Development is designed to explore the various economic and non-economic dimensions of development, construct universal notions of development that can be applied by individuals, organizations and governments globally for purposes of achieving development, which is conceptualized here as maturing. In this sense, although the so-called less developed countries have more development challenges, all countries are at different stages of development or maturity, and that respect is developing.

This Volume one introduces the Lecture Note Series on the Science of Development by briefly reviewing the commonly known theories and concepts of development. It is divided into eight chapters. Chapter one explains the difference and similarities between development and growth economics. Chapter two briefly surveys the contribution of Marxian economic thought to development. Rostow's stages of growth theory, the Harrod – Domar model, and Solow – Swan model are described in Chapters three, four, and five respectively. Joseph Schumpeter's theory of development is discussed in Chapter six. Chapter seven discusses development strategies, and lastly, Chapter eight explains poverty and inequality especially in less developed countries.

CHAPTER ONE

DEVELOPMENT AND GROWTH ECONOMICS

1.1. Growth Vs Development Economics

Economic growth is a sustained increase in the output of a state, region, or country over a short term, say a quarter, half-year, and 1 to 2 years. Whereas economic thinking is said to take place when an overall increase is experienced in the standard of living of a majority of people within a specified area (state, region or country). Development covers an increase in income and other aspects of wellbeing, especially health, education, security, and governance. More generally, growth economics studies the long-run, steady-state, equilibrium growth paths of fairly advanced or fast advancing countries (that is, middle to high-income countries). Growth economics is more relevant for countries where the majority of the population has advanced beyond the low incomes and thus having the larger proportion of its population in the middle and high-income classes. In other words, growth theories are more relevant for economies that are well developed or modernized, and have a large number of successful businesses and entrepreneurs, operating within responsive and highly functional systems incentives, institutions, and capabilities to drive the growth mechanism.

Typically, therefore, growth economics concerns the study and analyses of macroeconomic relationships, especially the ratio of savings to total output and the aggregate capital-output ratio as articulated in the Harrod-Domar and Solow-Swan models, and their derivatives. The fixed capital-output ratio adopted by the leading growth theories assumes away the vital facts or causes of underdevelopment, namely; ignorance, low capital absorption, low savings, and weak capacity to invest productively. The use of growth theories to analyze the situation of lee developed countries is thus generally faulty. For example, less developed countries can achieve growth by raising agricultural or mineral resources exports while the quality of social services and living conditions generally remains poor. Allocation of available savings among competing expenditure sub-heads may not support future growth due to corruption and poor governance. Poor governance may equally slow down the discovery of gainful investment options, low supply of incentives and support to entrepreneurs, and weak organizational framework in the private and public sectors.

1.2. Development Economics

Modern development thinking became popular after World War II when an increasing number of former colonies gained independence. The common claim made by leaders of independence movements was that colonialism skewed the distribution of income in favor of the colonists and their indigenous collaborators. The distribution inequities against the low income/poor class led to low incomes, and low income to low savings, low savings led to low investment, and low investment leads back to low income; thus completing the so-called vicious cycle of poverty. However, the pragmatic way out of the so-called vicious circle of poverty was capital importation for the fuller exploitation and exportation of natural resources so that the surpluses can be accumulated to the extent that the vicious circle is transformed to a virtuous circle of high savings leading to higher investment and then higher income. Thus inadvertently, early development studies used the logic of transforming the vicious circle of poverty to a virtuous circle of prosperity, via capital accumulation, to reconnect development thinking to growth theories which was primarily concerned with growth in income.

Thus although introduced because the assumption of growth economics failed to apply to underdeveloped or poor countries, early development models failed to emphasize or prioritize the non-income aspects of development. Addressing issues income distribution inequities was still a problem. It can be argued that since the 1950s when development thinking became popular, no known country can be said to have experienced speedy growth by applying any of the extant development theories. Since "shortage of capital" was considered the primary cause of underdevelopment, accelerating import substitution with capital importation and primary produce export proceeds was the path to development. Government was required to intervene actively in the functioning of the economy due to the high tendency for prices to fail in less developed countries.

Early development thinkers associated the process of development or economic advancement with industrialization, and poor countries were expected to benefit from technology spillovers from the advanced economies. Accordingly, terms like "catching up", "technology learning", "technology imitation" and "technology adoption" were popular lingoes of this era. More specifically, the early development thinkers attempted to explain underdevelopment with the following arguments, among other:

A. Effect of colonization

Colonial policies can impact positively or negatively on the future development of post-colonial states. For example, a colonial history that is characterized by massive displacement and cultural dislocation of the indigenous population, low technological learning by the local people, and low commitment to science and technology education in the host country will largely constrain development long after independence except deliberate steps are taken to hasten development. Generally French and British colonial rules have generally been disruptive of local development, compared to Japanese and German colonists.

B. The effect of cultural heterogeneity

Development may be faster where the population has either natural or constructed attributes that unify the people around common viewpoints or collective conscience. A common language, religion, and or a shared symbolism for patriotism can serve to nurture unifying rallying points. Equally a centralized state structure may help to promote or enhance development faster than decentralized or dispersed state structure.

C. Human capacity

A population that accesses education early is more likely to develop faster than those where education was accessed late. Even in the absence of formal education, early exposure to technical ongoing learning opportunities like apprenticeship system or mentoring can equally contribute to speedy development.

1.3. Globalization of development

From the 1970s development studies shifted from the preoccupation with capital accumulation and became generally associated with technological change and finding solutions to the specific problems faced by societies and countries. Countries had to design development strategies that suited their situation while in search of measures to hasten development. Development became more synonymous with continuing advancement that was needed by all the countries. In this globalized sense, modern development is conceptualized as the process of technology process (in power, transportation, healthcare, education, etc) and institutional change (such as the development of the market process, governance, international payment systems). Modern development thinking sees the entire globe as a developing space.

However, the perception that the poorer countries will need to do more to catch up with the advanced countries is still widely accepted. This is because countries and regions didn't initiate development at the same time and so some countries are ahead of others. At the same time, the diffusion of technological knowledge and skills from the advanced countries to the less advanced countries is not without several hitches that make it increasingly difficult for the poorer countries to learn, copy or steal technology from the advanced countries. Thus conventionally it is argued that poorer countries required more years to catch up, and that liberalized trade and the flow of foreign direct investment from the advanced to the less developed countries will speed up the technology learning process.

To enhance the technology learning process, the poorer countries are advised to first promote "light industries" (basically food and resources processing plants), after which they could progress to "secondary industries" (manufacture of consumables, basic furniture and other household wares, and so on) before proceeding to "tertiary industries", that is, production of machinery and precision goods, and growing services composites in all spheres of life. Given the huge investments and institutional changes required to move from one stage to another, it was believed that it will take long years for the poor or developing countries to move from the bio-mass dependence economies to having viable hi-tech (tertiary level) industries.

However, the experience of the so-called Asian Tigers - South Korea, Singapore, Indonesia, Malaysia, Singapore, Taiwan, and Thailand - over the period 1970 to 1990 showed that it was possible to leapfrog the 'dirty' stages and simultaneously modernize agriculture and manufacturing alongside developing hi-tech sophisticated industries. With the 'East Asian Miracle' the stage theories of development is now largely obsoleted. It is now the case that the development of countries lie in the determination of the people and the commitment and political will of their leaders.

1.4. Common Terms Used in Modern Development Studies

A. Underdeveloped Countries

Used commonly by Marxists and other radical economists to suggest that poorer countries have been made underdeveloped by richer countries. The underdevelopment hypothesis also suggests that poor countries are often unable to optimally utilize their potentials for economic growth and development. Development incapacities may be due to inadequate mineral and human resources, technological gaps, weak institutions, and low market potentials.

B. North and South Countries

The observed trend globally is that countries located in the Northern Hemisphere tend to be technologically more advanced than those in the Southern Hemisphere. It has equally become more common to have within countries and regions, the population group in the North dominate those in the South.

C. Third World

This term was commonly used during the Cold War era where the advanced or the most affluent Western (capitalist) countries were described as the "First World." The fast advancing countries were the "Second World" countries, while the less developed countries largely in Asia, Africa and Latin America are described as "Third World" countries.

CHAPTER TWO

MARXISM AND DEVELOPMENT

2.1. The Forces of Production

Marx viewed human history as being characterized by the evolution of the productivity of labor (the forces of production) in relation to the changing social structure within which production takes place (the social relations of production). The forces of production evolves historically, although at varying speeds depending on whether the social relations create a favorable or unfavorable climate for material progress. At key moments the forces of production find themselves held back by the form of society and this creates pressure for the revolutionary transitioning from one social system to another, for instance from feudalism to capitalism. This continuing evolutionary process plays a pivotal role in the development of human history.

Marx believes that what drives the historical societal evolutionary process is the pursuit of profit under competitive conditions, which impels an acceleration in the continuing transformation of productive forces from the level where competencies are generally absent, to higher levels of hi-tech mastery and sophistication. However, the ability to raise productivity endlessly that competition renders compelling is as well associated with growing inequality, where the number of people advancing into the affluent class is increasingly smaller than those remaining in the highly impoverished class. Capitalism, and its driving force competition, promotes the creation of a uniquely unequal system and polarizing of the population into a minority of affluent persons and a majority of propertyless poor.

Marxism generally envisions a human society that is advancing scientifically and materially, while at the same time continuing up a progressive movement from the primitive stage to the most advanced stage of capitalism, and thereafter a revolutionary transitioning to communism. Marx regarded capitalism as a system that is abhorrent because it rests on exploitation and generates inequality but is historically supportive of speedy advancement because it brings about an unprecedented development of the productive forces and creates its own "gravediggers", the property less working class.

However, in the decades following World War II, some Marxists began to argue that capitalism was no longer capable of producing economic development in the poorer parts of the world. Instead it would create growing polarization between the developed and underdeveloped countries. Pro-Marxian theories of inevitable polarization were already circulating among Latin American intellectuals when Paul Baran in the 1950s presented an explicitly Marxist version of it, concluding that "the capitalist system, once a mighty engine of economic development, has turned into a no less formidable hurdle to economic advancement" The cause of the onset of monopoly capital, a new stage of the system characterized a general tendency in the major centers' of capitalism to experience under consumption and crisis, that can only be checked by massive state spending, militarism and the exploitation of ethnic minorities and economically backward countries. Other theorists of polarization, by contrast, saw it as a process which had lasted through the four centuries of existence of a worldwide market, through which a privileged group of countries in the center could transfer resources from the dominated countries of the periphery through plunder, unequal trade and later investment and indebtedness. Particularly influential were the writings of Andre Gunder Frank, Immanuel Wallerstein, and Samir Amin etc.

2.2. The Importance of Ideology to Development

The impact of Marxian thinking on mainstream development thought is often ignored or downplayed by several pro-Western authors. But an honest review would indicate that proliferation of human centered development paradigms and indicators (such as, the basic needs approach and the United Nations Human Development Index (HDI)) was significantly motivated by the speed that that the then Soviet bloc countries and China developed. More specifically More specifically Marx emphasized the importance of ideology to development and how they are formed.. In the Marxian perspective, it is the dominant ideology or mental structure (not financial or material capital) that defines how a society confronts its fundamental economic problems. A good ideology is one that ensures that the forces of production is balanced with the system's ability to reproduce itself. Major contradictions are created when the forces of production (efficiency and productivity of labor and other production factors) grow faster than the ability of the people to keep buying and at the same time stay productive. In effect, seeking to continually increase production not minding the wellbeing of workers and their purchasing power is what causes the mismatch of the productive forces and the system's ability to reproduce itself.

For Marx the capitalist economies are unstable because of the conflict between the growth of the forces of production and the growth in the society's ability to reproduce itself. The problem is not just about capitalism, all modern economies have the tendency to take this balance for granted, and hence the widening gap between the affluent class and the low class globally. This mismatch is structural, and it takes continuing monitoring and deliberate compensatory activities to correct it.

2.2.1. Material Vs Idealistic Determinism

In the view of Marx, material necessity determines social being, and social being determines social consciousness. Thus the dominant human thoughts and ideologies are shaped by the means and processes of subsistence (the economic base), which in turn determines a population's worldview and social relations. Thus it is the concrete material facts that shapes ideology, and material consciousness is developed before social consciousness. In the Marxian perspective, for instance, poverty occurs because fewer persons in the society are able to access the level of income (and vital material assets and opportunities) they require to meet their vital needs. Poverty (or material lack) then shapes their sense of self-worth and world view.

Marx's materialist determinism contrast sharply with the much earlier opinion of Hegel, which is that is the sense of self-worth and world view that determines people's ability to access or achieve material successes. In contrast to the Marxian materialist dialectics, Hegel's idealistic dialectics submits that poverty is first and foremost a mental deficit before translating to a material lack. People are poor because of the mental pictures that they hold about themselves. The universe has all the resources that is needed in the state of consciousness and all that is required is for the individual/society to be attuned to what they need consciously and appropriate them. For Hegel therefore, the quality of mental pictures held precedes the material condition experienced. So while Hegel moves from the mental condition (social consciousness) to the material conditioning, Marx moves from the material condition to the mental conditioning.

In Hegel's dialectical idealism, truth is the product of history, and history a product of the "spirit of the time", and thought precedes matter. Ideologies are paradigms built up over generation. Arising from this some cultures/families have imbibed a cultures that support wealth creation, which generally influences their worldview and social consciousness. So for them, material lack can become an opportunity to strategize and accumulate wealth. But people whose minds are shaped by cultures that see material lack as limiting condition may begin to blame others for their problems. Following Hegel's idealism, it is possible to reshape the attitude to work and life of a people with constructed transformational ideology much the same as Mao Zedong and Lenin did for China and Russia respectively. We can thus take Hegel's idealism as the universal view, and the Marxian materialist idealism as applicable where the population are being trapped by poverty and being under conditions of extreme deprivation are unable to have confidence in their sense of self-worth and faith that they system can help them. This is similar to the liquidity trap thesis of John Maynard Keynes.

By the above reasoning the Marxian materialism and Hegel's idealism can be reconciled. While for Marx, under conditions where survival is threatened matter or material condition precedes thought. An individual facing the threat of dying from hunger will do anything possible to survive. In such special situations where the reserve army of the unemployed face life-threatening hunger, matter precedes thought, and as Marx noted, all phenomena in the universe are perceived as consisting of "matter in motion". But Hegel's view emphasizes the power and role of indoctrination (whether forcefully or gently using mental colonization) that may cause people to change their conduct regardless of the material base.

Fredric Engel extended Marxism to the global scene, where capital is internationalized and the power shifts from local capitalists to large multinational firms who exploit the working class and the less development countries from where they draw cheap resources to develop the center countries where their businesses are headquartered. This transnational exploitation of resource rich less developed countries by the developed countries, using the agency of MNCs, is what Engel refers to as imperialism.

Neither Marx nor Engel foresaw today's converging ideologies. In most developing and advanced countries, citizens and civil society organizations have become increasingly demanding, and putting serious pressure of the governments adopt implement far-reaching welfare measures. There are no longer capitalist and socialist countries as known or defined in theory. What we have now are hybrid systems all emphasizing growing need to pacify the population with welfare support measures. Clearly globalization of information and ideas are merging cultures and ideologies globally. Arthur (2000) opines that Marx's insufficient grasp of Hegel's philosophy may have accounted for his pre-occupation with materialist determinism, arguing further that Marx never explained his own method adequately because he was uncertain himself, especially about its relationship with Hegel's method, and indeed that Marx was confused about the relevance of Hegel's logic.

2.3. Economic Development Vs Development

Development, the activity that ensure a comprehensive improvement in the overall wellbeing of a population is a more universal concept; economic development has to be seen rightly an aspect of it and not necessary equated to it. It can be argued further that the colonization of human thinking by economics is largely responsible for the contradictions, distortions, and environmental degradation of today's world. Unperceived by many, the global community has accepted two assumptions of economics, namely non-satiation and scarcity as existential facts have rapped their thinking and actions around them. Firstly, non-satiation is used by economic agents/actors – individuals, organizations, and government - to justify greed and urge to accumulate more wealth often at the expense of others. Secondly, the assumption of scarcity puts economic agents in the survival mode such that they continually see themselves as fighting for survival regardless of the level of wealth that they have already. Thus economics serves as the unread 'Bible' that justifies excessive profit-seeking, capital accumulation, individualism, unbridled competition, and adoption of material wealth to the quintessential measure of success. Economics justifies the pursuit for wealth regardless of what one already and how such pursuit would impact human lives. Material pursuit is used to justify the proliferation in arms and ammunition, drug dealing and other destructive high-profit spinning activities.

2.3.1. Lessons from China's experiences

China's recent global emergence and sustained growth demonstrate how creating the appropriate social consciousness can promote self-sustaining development. From 1949 to 1976, Mao's ideology was the dominant influence on Chinese economic policies. In the ten years prior to his death (1966 to 1976), his ideology could be likened to a state religion. Several features of Maoism need to be kept in mind. Firstly, Mao believed that people, through sheer human willpower, could accomplish practically any end, and if properly mobilized, human resources were more important to economic development than capital or technology. Secondly, Mao believed in the primacy of social consciousness and social relations over the material or economic condition. In other words, Mao considered ideas, knowledge, information, and indoctrination as critical change factors. Thirdly, Mao constructed and popularized an ideology of the "communist man" which contrasts with selfishness, individualism, and egoism of the "economic man" adopted in mainstream Western economics.

Fourthly, unlike Stalin in Russia that forcefully imposed communism using collectivization, Mao first socialized many Chinese around the phenomenon of the "communist man" before proceeding to collectivization. With social change preceding collectivization, Maoism became a sort of religion, with Mao as the *high priest* and *Messiah*; making it less difficult for its believers to fight for its preservation years after Mao's death. This doctrine of Mao is the foundation of modern Chinese patriotism and social relations. For instance, it is common to see the Chinese form and operate a sustainable business and social partnerships; they live and eat in groups and have less interest in the accumulation of individual wealth in contrast with what obtains in western societies. Fifthly, Mao believed that equal distribution of income was at least as important as economic growth. Sixthly, Mao saw a continuing tendency to revert to capitalism that should be fought continually; making the revolution in a permanent state of flux. This means the society must continue orientating the people around the desired dominant mental structures and world view.

2.3.2. Lessons from the experience of the Defunct Soviet Union

The former Soviet Union was the best example of a prototype communist economy from its inception in 1918 until its collapse in 1991. Upon taking power in the Soviet Union in 1929, Stalin prophetically announced that Russia had ten years to overcome 100 years of backwardness if it wished to survive. In order to industrialize quickly, the focus was on "heavy industry". This required that the government have considerable control over the economy through a highly centralized Communist Party. In the former Soviet Union, all enterprises (and all land) were owned by the government, and their managers were bureaucrats. The passion to meet production targets had two limitations: firstly, the managers had no incentives to increase production beyond the targets because exceeding the target this year would certainly mean an increase in the planned target the next year; secondly, it made enterprise managers very resistant to change and innovation.

There were also incentives for enterprise managers to push for enterprise expansion. This encouraged managers of Soviet enterprises to ask for more funds for new capital goods than they actually needed. This phenomenon called *"investment hunger"* was also dysfunctional for at least two reasons. First, the government permitted the buying or building of more capital goods than it could possibly afford; often allowing many projects to remain partially completed for years. Second, enterprises became too large, leading to diseconomies of scale. This passion for very large companies has been called *"Gigantomania"*. Centralized planning led to certain dysfunctional behaviors; enterprise managers desiring easy targets and plentiful supplies distorted information. Enterprises commonly hired people to go around the country and bribe the directors of other enterprises in order to obtain needed materials. There were also problems with the unit of measurement of the production targets.

Agriculture was collectivized in a very bloody and destructive manner in the 1930s. Soviet agricultural production rarely reached the goals of the planners. Indeed, the growth rate of agricultural production was quite low by any standard. But the Soviet government tried to extract savings from farmworkers through high taxes for investment in the industry. This rendered agricultural infrastructure generally poor.

In the former Soviet Union, prices were in most cases set below market-level prices and were rarely changed. The result was shortages of most consumer goods. The pervasiveness of shortages led to forced savings, referred to as *"monetary overhang"*. This means that people had income but could not find anything to spend it on. A shortage economy created and sustained black markets and bribery of government officials became a fact of everyday life.

The Soviet Union had a policy of "autarky" which resulted from the government seeing other countries as "the enemy". Imports were limited to those necessary goods that could not be produced at home. Exports, mainly from agriculture, were to earn money to pay for imports. Transactions involving foreign exchange were tightly controlled by the government. The price charged for a good within the Soviet Union and the price charge in international trade had virtually no relation to each other. Production slowed generally until the mid-1980s when production in the Soviet Union may not have been growing at all. By the last half of the 1980s, Mikhail Gorbachev introduced *perestroika*, meaning restructuring. Perestroika only made marginal changes in the economy and between 1985 and 1989, the budget deficit more than doubled. In response, many of the changes of perestroika were reversed, which was an admission of failure. In August of 1991, communism collapsed completely after a failed coup against Gorbachev by hard-liner party members.

2.4. Marxism in Contemporary Development Thought

As discussed above, Marxism has added value to several aspects of contemporary economic thought.

In addition to its emphasis on ideologies, the Marxian dialectical materialism has several parallels with the Keynesian liquidity trap thesis. Equally important is Marx's explanation of how capitalists mask exploitation through the objectivistic separation of labor-power and labor-time. The labor hired or paid for is far less than the full expression of a worker's capacity to produce. The worker is made to see his labor as merely a mechanical means to an end; which are the wages that are often not enough to meet his/her needs. This separation makes the worker ignorant of the actual value of his/her contribution to the total product and hence lacks the legal basis to demand more reward than the meager amount they are paid. The capitalist system ensures that the value of labor power each worker puts into the production process far exceeds the labor time for which he/she is remunerated. Marx also focused on how exploitation can dialectically cause the capitalist economy to collapse: exploitation causes workers to be impoverished leading to a fall in aggregate demand and decline in the rate of profit; falling rate of profit causes employers to lay-off workers and intensify labor exploitation; workers and peasants become violent and demand the revolutionary overthrow of capitalism, and the capitalist system is ultimately overthrown and replaced with a more equitable system.

The real message of Marx is that an economic system that venerates material accumulation is both logically unsustainable and immoral, and more seriously, that workers in capitalist organizations are often paid far less than the value of their marginal product. It follows too that capitalism generally promotes the condition where workers remain poorly motivated to engage in serious reasoning, or reflect on issues beyond the received logic and morality of mercantilism. The workers' intellect is systematically separated from the ability to reason; one no longer implies the other, and reasoning tends to lag behind particularly in the developing world where the infrastructure for learning is poor. Marx describes the gap between growth in intellectualism and reasoning as the separation of substantive reality from objective reality, which can occur regardless of whether capitalism collapses or not.

An unintended consequence of labor exploitation that follows from Marx's argument is how the subversive activities of workers can cause the rate of profit to fall. Workers who rationally expect to be exploited by capitalists often take subversive steps to protect their buying power through theft, fraud, insider abuses, and other activities that affect the profitability of their employers (whether government or capitalist firms). This can explain sundry corrupt practices, insider abuses, and moral hazards that have caused the collapse or bankruptcy of capitalist firms and governments in recent years. Doubtlessly, Marx could not foresee today's knowledge societies where exploitation occurs largely in the context of mental colonization.

CHAPTER THREE

ROSTOW'S STAGES OF GROWTH THEORY

Rostow's Stages of Growth model was published by American economist Walt Whitman Rostow in 1960. It postulates that economic growth occurs in five basic stages, of varying length, namely; traditional society, preconditions for take-off, take-off, drive to maturity, and age of high mass consumption.

- **Traditional society** - primary sector economy, with limited technology, and a high level of resistance to change.

- **Pre-conditions to "take-off"** - external demand for raw material exports initiates economic change. This stage is more specifically characterized by the following:
  a. Widespread development of infrastructures that support primary

production e.g. irrigation, canals, ports.

b. Spread of processing technology and other advances in existing technologies.

c. Changing social structures and equilibriums.

d. Breakdown of customary inhibitions

e. And, development of group identities based of nationalistic or economic interests.

- **Take off** – this era is characterized by faster rates of urbanization and industrialization, technological breakthroughs, growth in secondary production as happened in Great Britain's classic "Industrial Revolution".

- **Drive to maturity** – this stage is characterized by the following:
    1. Diversification of the industrial base - multiple industries expand and new ones take root quickly;
    2. Production of capital goods and machines;

3. Production of local consumables;

4. Development of infrastructures for transportation and other large-scale investment in other social infrastructure (schools, universities, hospitals, etc.).

- **Age of mass consumption** - industrial output dominates the economy as the primary sector diminishes quickly. Growth in the value and quality of local consumer goods. More people are able to consume beyond the bare needs of subsistence.

3.1. Implications of Rostow's Model

Countries go through each of these stages fairly linearly, and the investment portfolio continues to change. The stages and transition periods may differ slightly from country to country. Rostow's model, like other classical economic models, emphasized the efficacy of free trade, and disagree with the view that economies relying on exports of raw materials may get "locked-in", and would not be able to diversify. Rostow's model does not disagree with Keynes regarding the importance of government control over domestic development which is not generally accepted by some ardent free-trade advocates. Rostow's model is criticized for being mechanical by assuming that development in "newcomer countries will follow the pattern of today's advanced economies. However, the fact of today's development is that several countries are increasingly able to skip the stages by simultaneously developing all sectors.

CHAPTER FOUR

HARROD-DOMAR MODEL

Harrod-Domar model was developed independently by Roy F. Harrod in 1939, and Evsey Domar in 1946. Harrod–Domar model identifies three kinds of growth, namely; warranted growth, actual growth, and the natural rate of growth.

- Harrod–Domar (H-D) model was initially created to help analyze the business cycle, and later adapted to explain economic growth. It implies that growth depends on the quantity of labor and capital and that more investment leading to capital accumulation is required to generate economic growth.

- Less Developed Countries (LDCs) with plentiful low-skilled labor (earning low income) and low level of physical capital would experience slowing economic progress. In other words, LDCs do not have sufficiently high incomes for the required rates of saving, and the accumulation of physical capital stock through investment is low.

- The model implies that economic growth depends on policies to increase investment, by increasing saving and using that investment more efficiently through technological advances. The model concludes growth is a deliberate process involving continuing accumulation of investment, and that an economy does not "naturally" find full employment and stable growth rates.

- H-D model is widely criticized for assuming the fixed relative price of labor and capital. Equally, the assumption that investors are only influenced by output growth (or the accelerator principle) has been found not to be true in all cases.

- The H-D model is also criticized for seeing economic development and growth as the same, while in reality economic growth is only a subset of development. More seriously, the model implies that poor countries should necessarily borrow to finance growth without giving due consideration to challenges of repayment.

4.1. Mathematical Presentation

Let Y represent output, which equals income, K is capital stock. S is total saving, s is the savings rate, and I is an investment. δ stands for the rate of depreciation of the capital stock. The H-D model makes the following *a priori* assumptions:

$$Y = f(K)$$

1: Output is a function of capital stock

$$\frac{dY}{dK} = c \Rightarrow \frac{dY}{dK} = \frac{Y}{K}$$

2: The marginal product of capital is constant; the production function exhibits constant returns to scale. This implies capital's marginal and average products are equal.

$$f(0) = 0$$

3: Capital is necessary for output.

$$sY = S = I$$

4: The product of the savings rate and output equals saving, which equals investment

$$\Delta K = I - \delta K$$

5: The change in the capital stock equals investment less the depreciation of the capital stock

Using dots (for example, $\dot{Y}$) to denote percentage growth rates.

First, assumptions (1)–(3) imply that output and capital are linearly related, that is, capital-elasticity of output is equal to 1.

These assumptions thus generate equal growth rates between the two variables. That is,
$$Y = cK \Rightarrow d\log(Y) = d\log(c) + d\log(K).$$

Since the marginal product of capital, c, is a constant, we have
$$d\log(Y) = d\log(K) \Rightarrow \frac{dY}{Y} = \frac{dK}{K} \Rightarrow \dot{Y} = \dot{K}.$$

Next, with assumptions (4) and (5), we can find capital's growth rate as,
$$\dot{K} = \frac{I}{K} - \delta = s\frac{Y}{K} - \delta$$
$$\Rightarrow \dot{Y} = sc - \delta$$

In sum, the savings rate times the marginal product of capital minus the depreciation rate equals the output growth rate. Increasing the savings rate, increasing the marginal product of capital, or decreasing the depreciation rate will increase the growth rate of output; these are the means to achieve growth in the Harrod–Domar model.

CHAPTER FIVE

SOLOW–SWAN MODEL

This is an exogenous long-run neoclassical economic growth model. The growth drivers of the Solow-Swan (S-S) model are capital accumulation, labor or population growth, and increases in productivity (technological progress). The S-S model is founded on the aggregate production function, typically the Cobb-Douglas, which gives it microeconomic foundation. The model was developed independently by Robert Solow and Trevor Swan in 1956 as improvements over the H-D model. Solow extended the H-D model by adding labor as a factor of production, and the capital-labor ratios are not fixed as they are in the H–D model. These refinements allow increasing capital intensity to be distinguished from technological progress. The key assumption of the neoclassical growth model is that capital is subject to diminishing returns in a closed economy.

Major short-run implications of the S-S model are as follows:

- Policy measures like tax cuts or investment subsidies can affect the level of output but not the rate of output growth.

- Changes in savings rates only affect growth rates in the short-run while the economy converges to the new steady-state level of output.

- The rate of growth while the economy converges to the steady-state is determined by the rate of capital accumulation.

- Capital accumulation is in turn determined by the savings rate (the proportion of output used to create more capital rather than being consumed) and the rate of capital depreciation.

- The long-run implications of the S-S model are as follows:

    1. Long run rate of growth is exogenously determined. This means that long-run growth depends on the rate of labor force growth. In the steady-state, a country with a high savings rate and a country with a low savings rate will experience the same rate of growth in output/worker.

2. The model predicts that poor countries will grow rapidly if they raise the share of output (GDP) they invest in capital. When this happens the Solow-Swan model predicts that economic growth per worker will converge to the lower, steady-state rate determined by technological progress.

- In the Solow-Swan model the unexplained change in the growth of output after accounting for the effect of capital accumulation is called the Solow residual. This residual measures the exogenous increase in total factor productivity (TFP) during a particular time period.

- Increase in TFP is often attributed to technological progress, but it also includes any permanent improvement in the efficiency with which factors of production are combined over time. The model can be reformulated in slightly different ways using different productivity assumptions, or different measurement metrics.

5.1. Mathematics of the S-S Model

Typically, the S-S model is set in continuous-time world with no government or international trade. Output is produced using two factors of production, labor (L) and capital (K) in a Cobb-Douglas type production function.

$$Y(t) = K(t)^\alpha (A(t)L(t))^{1-\alpha}$$

Where t denotes time, $0 < \alpha < 1$ is the elasticity of output with respect to capital, and $Y(t)$ represents total production.

- A refers to labor-augmenting technology or "knowledge", thus AL represents effective labor. All factors of production are fully employed, and initial values $A(0)$, $K(0)$, and $L(0)$ are given.

- A The number of workers, i.e. labor, as well as the level of technology grow exogenously at rates n and g, respectively:

$$L(t) = L(0)e^{nt}$$

$$A(t) = A(0)e^{gt}$$

The number of effective units of labor, $A(t)L(t)$, therefore grows at rate $(n+g)$.

Meanwhile, the stock of capital depreciates over time at a constant rate δ. However, only a fraction of the output ($cY(t)$ with $0 < c < 1$) is consumed, leaving a saved share $s = 1 - c$ for investment:

$$\dot{K}(t) = sY(t) - \delta K(t)$$

where $\dot{K}$ is shorthand for $\dfrac{dK(t)}{dt}$, the derivative with respect to time. Derivative with respect to time means that it is the change in capital stock— output that is neither saved nor used to replace worn-out old capital goods is net investment.

Since the production function $Y(K, AL)$ has constant returns to scale, it can be written as output per effective unit of labor:

$$y(t) = \frac{Y(t)}{A(t)L(t)} = k(t)^\alpha$$

The main interest of the model is the dynamics of capital intensity k, the capital stock per unit of effective labor. Its behavior over time is given by the key equation of the Solow–Swan model:

$$\dot{k}(t) = sk(t)^\alpha - (n + g + \delta)k(t)$$

The first term, $sk(t)^\alpha = sy(k(t))$, is the actual investment per unit of effective labor: the fraction s of the output per unit of effective labor

$y(k(t))$ that is saved and invested. The second term $(n+g+\delta)k(t)$, is the "break-even investment": the amount of investment that must be invested to prevent k from falling.

The equation implies that $k(t)$ converges to a steady-state value of k^*, defined by $sk(t)^\alpha = (n+g+\delta)k(t)$, at which there is neither an increase nor a decrease of capital intensity:

$$k^* = \left(\frac{s}{n+g+\delta}\right)^{\frac{1}{1-\alpha}}$$

at which the stock of capital K and effective labor AL are growing at rate $(n+g)$

By assumption of constant returns, output Y is also growing at that rate. In essence, the Solow–Swan model predicts that an economy will converge to a balanced-growth equilibrium, regardless of its starting point. In this situation, the growth of output per worker is determined solely by the rate of technological progress.

Since $\alpha < 1$, at any time t the marginal product of capital $K(t)$ in the Solow-Swan model is inversely related to the capital/labor ratio.

$$MPK = \frac{\partial Y}{\partial K} = \alpha A^{1-\alpha}/(K/L)^{1-\alpha}$$

If productivity A is the same across countries, then countries with less capital per worker have a higher marginal product, which would provide a higher return on capital investment.

As a consequence, the model predicts that in a world of open market economies and global financial capital, investment will flow from rich countries to poor countries, until capital/worker ratio and income/worker ratio equalize across countries.

5.2. Mankiw–Romer–Weil Version S-S Model

N. Gregory Mankiw, David Romer, and David Weil created a human capital augmented version of the S-S model that can explain the failure of international investment to flow to poor countries. In this model output and the marginal product of capital (K) are lower in poor countries because they have less human capital than rich countries. For simplicity, they assume the same function of accumulation for both types of physical and human capital.

The Mankiw, Romer, and Weil model provides a lower estimate of the TFP (residual) than the basic Solow-Swan model because the addition of human capital to the model enables capital accumulation to explain more of the variation in income across countries. The Solow-Swan model augmented with human capital predicts that the income levels of poor countries will tend to catch up with or converge towards the income levels of rich countries if the poor countries have similar savings rates for both physical capital and human capital as a share of output, a process known as conditional convergence. However, savings rates vary widely across countries. In particular, since considerable financing constraints exist for investment in schooling, savings rates for human capital are likely to vary as a function of cultural and ideological characteristics in each country.

CHAPTER SIX

JOSEPH SCHUMPETER'S THEORY OF DEVELOPMENT

Schumpeter's perspective on economic development assigns the most significant role to entrepreneurship with its inseparable and embedded innovative nature. The transient character of the economic function performed by entrepreneurs makes impossible the formation of a social class in a typical way, but a large number of those who have carried out successful innovation belong to the class of capitalists. More seriously, engagement in entrepreneurial activities is an excellent mechanism for upward social mobility, to the achievement of higher social status for the individual and his or her family. In Schumpeter's view, the entrepreneur can be a very discrete person who need not convince others from the market about 'the desirability' of his or her vision, capacities, or abilities because he or she can move the means of production into the desired channels; the only entity to convince or impress is the financier. Schumpeter's view cannot be dissociated from entrepreneurial action. Indeed, Schumpeter believes that the entrepreneur is typically a debtor, and capital is the lever by which the entrepreneur diverts the factors of production to new uses, and dictates the direction to production. The entrepreneurial activity is distinct from the routine administration of a firm; the entrepreneur need not directly run the business.

Schumpeter's metaphor of 'creative destruction' is embedded in the role attributed to the entrepreneur and innovation. Schumpeter's theory of development assigns a paramount role to the entrepreneur and innovations introduced. The process of production is marked by a combination of material and immaterial productive forces. The material productive forces arise from the traditional factors of production; that is, land and labor, while the immaterial productive forces are conditioned on technological and social change. Schumpeter regarded land to be constant, and growth as coming from in population and increase in the producer goods. Savings and accumulation arise profits that are due to innovations such as new techniques of production or new product introduced. In Schumpeter's view, expansion of output depends upon the history of technological development. In simple terms, Schumpeter believes that the growth of output is geared to the rate of innovations, and the entrepreneur plays a key role. Generally, innovation consists in: (1) introduction of anew good; (2) introduction of a new method of production; (3) the opening of a new market; (4) the discovery of a new source of supply of raw materials or semi-manufactured goods; and (5) introduction of a new organization in an industry. The entrepreneur needs exceptional ability and daring will to deal with a high degree of risk and uncertainty. Typically, he/she is not lured by profit alone but also by a desire to grow a business and compete globally. Moreover, entrepreneurs do better in societies where they are honored and prestige is attached to them.

Another new point introduced by Schumpeter in this analysis of economic development is the important role that credit plays in economic development. The credit is not from saving out of current income but through credit created by the banking system. Thus, Schumpeter makes credit creation an integral part of the development. However, Schumpeter notes that the dominance of the entrepreneur or the producer limits and reduces correspondingly the sovereignty of the consumer. The producer can using advertising and design thinking move to consumer to accept what is being produced. By his dynamic role, through high pressure of salesmanship, he attempts and succeeds fairly in changing even the tastes of consumers or in creating in them new wants and desires. Also unlike the neoclassical economists who believed that the process of economic development was gradual and harmonious, Schumpeterian analysis shows that economic growth is characterized by uneven and disharmonious spurts and leaps and bounds.

More generally, three major factors distinguish Schumpeterian analyses from the Marxian analyses: (a) Schumpeter identifies interest rate as a determinant of savings and an important factor in economic development; (b) he separates the autonomous investment from the induced investment and emphasizes dynamic impact of innovation as a determinant of autonomous investment; and (c) he regards entrepreneurship as the vital force which facilitates economic progress

Relevance of Schumpeter's Theory for Developing Countries:

1. Schumpeter's analysis of the entrepreneurial innovations does not appear to capture the fact that in today's world, the entrepreneur does not necessarily have to innovate. He can buy innovations and contract S&T experts to produce them. However, his view of development as spontaneous and discontinuous change is quite relevant now.

2. His analysis of how rigid and outmoded socio-economic institutions, low saving potential and laggard technology affect development adversely is quite correct. Also the role of foreign capital in technological progress when combined with good entrepreneurs is quite correct.

CHAPTER SEVEN

DEVELOPMENT STRATEGIES

7.1. Inward Vs Outward Looking development Strategies

The inward-looking strategy emphasizes trade protection and barriers to Foreign Direct Investment (FDI). The idea behind this strategy for development is to exploit forward and backward technological linkages. Associated with the inward looking perspective are various *catch-up hypotheses* like the early Japanese industrial policy of copying technologies developed in other countries and at the same time protect the infant industry through trade barriers. The outward-looking development strategy stresses the importance of international trade and FDI as levers for development. Advocates of this perspective usually argue in favor of free trade. A foreign policy by developing countries trying to remove these subsidies and barriers is an example of outward-looking development policy.

- The two types of outward-looking development policies are export promotion and import substitution.

- Export promotion strategies are based on the assumption that there are unemployed or dormant resources that can be put forward for exports at little or no cost. A major problem with this approach to development is that primary commodity export (except for oil and some rare minerals) are growing more slowly than total world trade.

- Import substitution can be seen as development through two stages: first, imported consumer goods are replaced by domestic production; and second, local production of more advanced products grows until the country becomes a net exporter.

7.2. Import Substitution Industrialization (ISI) Vs Export Promotion Strategy

The ISI strategy defines industrialization rather narrowly as attempting to produce locally what is currently imported. Capital was therefore identified with durable capital equipment in the form of complex machinery and other inputs that the underdeveloped countries were not able to produce domestically. Thus, foreign exchange requirements were calculated on the basis of the fixed technical input-output coefficients of the manufacturing sector. With high levels of protection for domestic industry, and with exchange rates that were often maintained at unrealistic levels (usually in an effort to make imported capital goods "cheap"), the experience of most developing countries was that export earnings grew relatively slowly. The simultaneously sharp increase in demand for imported capital goods (and for raw materials and replacement parts as well) resulted in unexpectedly large increases in imports. Most developing countries found themselves with critical foreign exchange shortages and were forced to reduce imports in order to cut fiscal deficits to manageable proportions.

The cutbacks in imports usually resulted in reduced growth rates, if not recessions. This result led to the view that economic stagnation was caused primarily by a shortage of foreign exchange with which to buy essential industrial inputs. But over the longer term the growth rates of countries that continued to protect their domestic industries heavily not only stagnated but declined sharply. Most countries relying on the ISI strategy experienced foreign-exchange shortages continually.

Export promotion strategies are necessary for stimulating economic development, especially in LDCs. Where foreign exchange scarcity is a major constraint to industrial growth, the government has to go beyond the conventional policy of eliminating the obstacles to the smooth functioning of market forces and aiding the export firms with information about the destination markets and foreign competitors. Other critical support areas may include: (1) to supporting export oriented firms with key limiting factors like packaging and logistics; (2) easing the internal documentation processes; (3) assisting leading export firms to access low-interest credits; (4) help them to source imported inputs required for the production of exported final products at lower cost; (5) undertake commercial diplomacy campaigns for exporting firms in the export destination countries; and more generally (6) provide the SMEs with a wide range of support since they make up a significant number of firms with promising export potentials.

A number of countries have export promotion councils. But going beyond that to create desks for export promotion in embassies and consulates can help the two way connecting of entrepreneurs in the host countries to the home countries and vis versa can go a long way to securing old markets and opening new ones. At the same time, inter-ministerial cooperation is needed to ensure that all of the government and the private sector are involved with the export-promoting drive. Indeed, a pre-condition for a successful Export Promotion Strategy (EPS) is the government's ability to mainstream export promotion in all its policies and programs.

The optimal mix of ISI and EPS is needed for a country to develop in a balanced way. There should be a deliberate effort to grow the capacity to produce some goods that are currently being imported, without necessarily having to ban the imports that are being substituted. At the same time targeting export markets for goods that are currently being produced and consumed locally is necessary for development sustainability.

7.3. The missing-Component Approach and Development Diagnostics

This set of theories regard shortage of some strategic input (such as the supply of savings, foreign exchange, or technical skills) as the main cause of underdevelopment, and once the missing component is supplied it is believed that economic development would follow in a predictable manner based on fixed quantitative relationships between input and output. Diagnosing the problem that a country has is necessary for missing links to be identified. Each country is unique and probably needs its specific strategy. Like a medical doctor, the development diagnostics framework applies a hierarchical procedure for testing different diagnoses to determine and isolate "illnesses". The economist is required to apply a "diagnostic tree" to identify different possible limitations to growth and afterward suggest treatments for the isolated "disease". Generally, the approach sets out from a postulate with a broad acceptance (what many people would agree), such as; that a high level of private investments and entrepreneurship are good and should be promoted by a development strategy. The most important contribution of "growth diagnostic", probably, is that it tells us that there is no medicine that can be used for all countries.

CHAPTER EIGHT

POVERTY AND INEQUALITY

The modern perspective on development focuses on how to assist societies to escape from absolute poverty and inequality. While bringing people out of poverty may not be an easy task to accomplish, all hands must be on deck to eliminate poverty for the following reasons:

- **Inequality is inefficient** - it reduces the income of the middle class and aggregate saving (the middle class has the highest propensity for saving). Investments reduce as only a few can provide the collateral necessary for getting loans. With regard to investments in human capital, inequality creates a bias towards higher education, while development often is better served by increased investments in higher quality primary and intermediate education.

- **Inequality destroys social capital** - mutual trust and reciprocity deplete and rent-seeking by a small elite using bribes and corruption promoted.

- **Inequality worsens poverty** - some economists argue that inequality compels people in the low-income class to work towards early flight from poverty. However, most poor persons cannot afford the basic needs for a healthy life required for sustaining hard work.

8.1. Poverty inducing Factors

Unemployment promotes poverty directly. In many countries also many persons in jobs are disguisedly unemployed because their marginal productivity is either too low or negative. Such labor can be withdrawn from the present activities to other activities without significant reduction in the productivity of the present activity. The failure of markets to support technology transfer can induce poverty. Market fundamentalists believe that development is a matter of transferring new technology from the developed countries and establish efficient institutions for securing free markets in the developing countries. New technologies can help poor countries leap frog dirty technologies, and governments need to take deliberate steps to promote technology transfer. It is widely accepted that the combination of market mechanism and direct government involvement in the economy through economic planning is required for uninterrupted economic development.

Government participation can take the form of public enterprises, public-private-partnerships (PPPs), and a variety of government regulatory and support programs. For example, price controls, import licensing, investment licenses, and capacity licenses can be used to regulate production, importation, and employment. The challenge in many LDCs is that government's ability to intervene is inhibited by sundry bottlenecks and corrupt practices. At the same time, public sector enterprises have generally not done well in developing countries due to corruption and other abuses. An optimal mix of government participation and the market process is required.

8.2. Poverty and the agrarian system in Africa

Modern studies of development indicate that developing countries are different and therefore have to be dealt with differently. Due to subdivision of land, there is a trend both in Asia and Africa that the sizes of individual farms are becoming smaller. Social and cultural institutions are crucial characteristics of an agrarian system. In the African system the allocation of control of resources depends on kinship both by descent and by marriage, implying that husband and wife usually have their own separate economy and the oldest son takes over the responsibility for the family after the father. Other characteristics of the African agrarian are the following:

- *Subsistence farming* - majority of farming families in Africa plan their output primarily for their own subsistence. Subsistence farming is threatened by scarcity of labour as fewer young persons are interested in farm work.

- *Outdated farming methods* – conservatism, inadequate extension services, and lack of other forms of support slows down technology adoption among the farmers in many LDCs. However, with a growing population, adopting agricultural intensification methods is necessary.

Reducing poverty is intimately connected to sustainable development, as on the one hand, poverty can promote environmental degradation, and on the other, poverty is and is itself a result of environmental degradation. Sustainable development requires that the stock of overall capital assets remain constant or rises over time. Many activities of the poor degrade the environment and produce downward spirals leading away from sustainable development. For example, poor people use firewood as their main source of energy, and the collection of firewood is sometimes made the scapegoat of deforestation. Furthermore, only a few poor persons add fertilizers and many cultivate marginal land. This creates a negative spiral as the well-being of the poor is further reduced because they must live on degraded land that is less expensive. Accordingly, transforming subsistence farming to mixed farming is a matter of identifying positive spirals, where measures reducing environmental degradation increase the well-being of the poor, which, in a second step, lead to further reductions in environmental degradation and so on. For example, the environment is conserved as more persons move up the energy ladder from firewood to charcoal, kerosene or better still solar energy.

However, the environmental Kuznets curve suggests that degradation increases when incomes increase and then decreases like an inverted U-curve. Since this curve describes the development of the whole society, it might well be that the non-poor increase the environmental degradation while environmental degradation by the poor decreases when income increases. The net effect may be negative. Poor farmers require support to adopt new technology such as using manufactured, synthetic fertilizer to improve the soil quality in a way that brings them from subsistence to mixed farming. Less costly methods for soil management that can replace slash-and-burn agriculture should be introduced. Equally, the soil management systems that promote conservation and renewal need to be introduced.